WORLD VISION EARLY READERS

I Like to Play

Marla Stewart Konrad

Tundra Books

Text and photographs copyright © 2010 by World Vision

All royalties from the sale of this book go to support World Vision's work with children.

Published in Canada by Tundra Books,
75 Sherbourne Street, Toronto, Ontario M5A 2P9

Published in the United States by
Tundra Books of Northern New York,
P.O. Box 1030, Plattsburgh, New York 12901

Library of Congress Control Number: 2009935196

Library and Archives Canada Cataloguing in Publication

Konrad, Marla Stewart
   I like to play / Marla Stewart Konrad.

(World Vision early readers)
ISBN 978-0-88776-998-6

   1. Play--Juvenile literature. I. World Vision Canada
II. Title. III. Series: World Vision early readers

GV182.9.K65 2009   j790.1'922   C2009-902995-2

We acknowledge the financial support of the Government of Canada through the Book Publishing Industry Development Program (BPIDP) and that of the Government of Ontario through the Ontario Media Development Corporation's Ontario Book Initiative. We further acknowledge the support of the Canada Council for the Arts and the Ontario Arts Council for our publishing program.

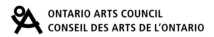

ONTARIO ARTS COUNCIL
CONSEIL DES ARTS DE L'ONTARIO

Printed and bound in China

1 2 3 4 5 6   15 14 13 12 11 10

Photo Credits:

Cover: Jon Warren, Sudan
Title Page: Alissa Bistonath , South Africa
Dedication Page: Pratigya Khaling, Nepal

Spreads:

At the Park: L - Sopheak Kong, Cambodia; TR - Zhang Jin, China;
   BR - Jon Warren, Sudan
Zoom/Fly: TL - Sarat Arias/Carols Brito, Dominican Republic;
   BL - David du Chemen, Ecuador; R - Andrew Goodwin, Bangladesh
Water Play: L - Jon Warren, Peru; TR - Jon Warren, Indonesia;
   BR - Ursula Meissner, Malawi
Homemade Toys: TL - Jon Warren, Sudan; BL - Jon Warren, Sudan;
   TR - Amio Ascension, Bangladesh; BR - Ursula Meissner, Malawi
Love to Dance: TL - Jon Warren, Peru; BL - Kevin Cook, Democratic
   Republic of Congo; TR - Lay Htoo, Myanmar; BR - Jon Warren,
   Indonesia
Jump/Skip/Hop: TL - Asanga Warnakulasuriya, Sri Lanka;
   BL - Michelle Tam, China; R - Paul Bettings, Democratic Republic
   of Congo
Friends: TL - Albert Yu, Laos; BL - Juan Miguel Lago, Philippines;
   TR - World Vision Photo, Armenia; BR - Sopheak Kong, Cambodia
Swing: Jon Warren, Honduras
Builders: TL - Jon Warren, Indonesia; BL - Lay Htoo, Myanmar;
   TR - Jerry Galea, Vietnam; BR - Philip Maher, Indonesia
Balls: TL - Jon Warren, Sudan; BL - Katie Chalk, Cambodia; TR - Justin
   Douglass, Mongolia; BR - Alyssa Bistonath, Ethiopia
Don't You?: Justin Douglass, Mongolia

For Larry, and for Aidan, Juliana, and Nathan.

I like to play, don't you? At the park I
play with my friends.

I can make my toys zoom very fast
or fly up to the sky.

Playing in water can be messy, but it is lots of fun!

When I do not have
anything to play with, I
can make my own toys.

My friends and I
love to dance.

Jump, skip, jump.
I can hop so high!

Friends to play with make
my day very happy.

On a swing, I glide through
the air. When I go high,
my tummy tickles.

It is hard work to be a builder.

On my own or with friends...

playing ball is great fun.

I like to play, don't you?